The Elements of San Joaquin

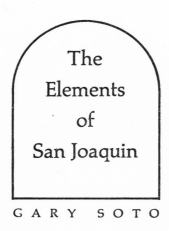

The
Elements
of
San Joaquin

G A R Y   S O T O

University of Pittsburgh Press

Published by the University of Pittsburgh Press, Pittsburgh, Pa. 15260
Copyright © 1977, Gary Soto
All rights reserved
Baker and Taylor International, London
Manufactured in the United States of America

Second printing 1980
Third printing 1986
Fourth printing 1989

Library of Congress Cataloging in Publication Data

Soto, Gary.
   The elements of San Joaquin.

   (Pitt poetry series)
   I. Title.
PS3569.O72E4   811'.5'4   76–26104
ISBN 0–8229–3335–7
ISBN 0–8229–5279–3 pbk.

"Telephoning God" first appeared in *Antaeus*, Winter 1976. "Copper" first appeared in *The North American Review*. Five sections of "The Elements of San Joaquin," "Avocado Lake," "October," and "Moving" first appeared in *Poetry*. "Moving Away" (p. 53): © 1976, The New Yorker Magazine, Inc. "Spirit" copyright © 1976 by P. R., Inc.

Other poems first appeared in *The American Poetry Review, Black Warrior Review, Graham House Review, Iowa Review, Marilyn, The Nation, Poetry Now,* and *Entrance: Four Chicano Poets* (Greenfield Review Press, 1976).

para mi Abuelita y mi Madre

Contents

.

1

San Fernando Road

para Leonard Cruz

On this road of factories
Gray as the clouds
That drifted
Above them,
Leonard was among men
Whose arms
Were bracelets
Of burns
And whose families
Were a pain
They could not
Shrug off.
He handled grinders,
Swept the dust
Of rubber
The wind peeled
Into the air
And into his nostrils,
Scrubbed the circles
From toilets
No one flushed.
Young Mexicans
Went into ovens
Squint-eyed
And pulled out the pipes
Smeared black
With tar.
Far from home,
He had no place
To go. Nights
He slept in cars

Or behind warehouses,
Shivering
Like the machinery
That went on and on.
And once,
While watching
The stars
And what might
Have been a cloud,
He did not think
Of the cousin
Spooning coke
Nor the woman
Opening
In her first rape,
But his body,
His weakening body,
And dawn only hours away.

The Underground Parking

para J. T.

A man who holds fear
Like the lung a spot of cancer,
Waits for your wife.
He is already listening for her whimper
To stop echoing and to break
Against concrete, listening
For the final fist at her ear,
For morning to arrive
Without the door tearing from its hinges.

The woman who gets it in a car
Or on the hard earth of a vacant lot,
Is under the heaviness of a toilet not flushing,
Of Out of a job and Why change
Bedsheets? She is under arms of tattoos,
Kick in the mouth, shitted shorts,
An ice pick at the throat.
She faces No rent money, Alice,
And not a single tear or a multitude could pull him off.

When his breath sours with fear,
And he cringes at the finger poking the doorbell,
I could give him the bread of my luck
And a prayer to go along—
If your fist closes, open it.
If you curse, swallow your tongue
Because you won't have nothing to say,
Not a kind word to lead him
From where he squats, waiting.

County Ward

It begins in a corridor. A woman phones
Her uncle good-bye, the roster for ping-pong
Goes unsigned.

It continues,
And Leon naps hugging his shoes.
When he wakens he asks for water,
For rain to come in one door and leave by another;
He asks for the song of a woman
And hears a broom stroke.

Then onto Rachel and Maria, the dull mothers,
Who bandage, sponge dirt from cheeks,
Saying: *Go sleep, baby.*

And always
The old one who runs through rooms, cafeteria;
He is a plane watching the horizon
Where his son disappeared.

*

There is a pain that gets up and moves, like the night attendant,
Pointing to the cough
That rises like dust and is dust
A month later, pointing to the blond one
Who bites a smile and strokes
Under blankets, under the guilt of the one light
That never blinks off.

It comes to speak in the drugged voice
That ate its tongue, the cane tapping
Its way from window to TV,
And back again.
                        Outside,
Left of the neon glowing *Eat,*
Right of the traffic returning home,
This cold slowly deepens
The old whose bones ring with the coming weather,
The black children buttoning and unbuttoning their coats,
The stunned face that could be your father's—
Deepens the gray space between each word
That reaches to say you are alone.

After Tonight

Because there are avenues
Of traffic lights, a phone book
Of brothers and lawyers,
Why should you think your purse
Will not be tugged from your arm
Or the screen door
Will remain latched
Against the man
Who hugs and kisses
His pillow
In the corridor of loneliness?

There is a window of light
A sprinkler turning
As the earth turns,
And you do not think of the hills
And of the splintered wrists it takes
To give you
The heat rising toward the ceiling.

You expect your daughter
To be at the door any moment
And your husband to arrive
With the night
That is suddenly all around.
You expect the stove to burst
A collar of fire
When you want it,
The siamese cats
To move against your legs, purring.

But remember this:
Because blood revolves from one lung to the next,
Why think it will
After tonight?

Telephoning God

for Jon Veinberg

Drunk in the kitchen, I ring God

And get Wichita,
Agatha drunk and on the bed's edge, undoing
Her bra.

Dial again, and Topeka comes through like snoring,
Though no one sleeps. Not little Jennifer
Yelling "But Mommy,"
                        nor Ernie kissing
The inside of his wrist, whispering
"This is a Gorgeous Evening."

Dial again, and only the sound of spoons crashing
In a cafeteria in Idaho,

A little silence, then a gnat circling the ear
Of Angela beaten and naked in the vineyard,
Her white legs glowing.

The Morning They Shot Tony Lopez, Barber and Pusher Who Went Too Far, 1958

When they entered through the back door,
You were too slow in raising an arm
Or thinking of your eyes refusing the light,
Or your new boots moored under the bed,
Or your wallet on the bureau, open
And choking with bills,
Or your pockets turned inside out, hanging breathless as tongues,
Or the vendor clearing his throat in the street,
Or your watch passed on to another's son,
Or the train to Los Banos,
The earth you would slip into like a shirt
And drift through forever.
When they entered, and shot once,
You twisted the face your mother gave
With the three, short grunts that let you slide
In the same blood you closed your eyes to.

2

The Elements of San Joaquin

Field

The wind sprays pale dirt into my mouth
The small, almost invisible scars
On my hands.

The pores in my throat and elbows
Have taken in a seed of dirt of their own.

After a day in the grape fields near Rolinda
A fine silt, washed by sweat,
Has settled into the lines
On my wrists and palms.

Already I am becoming the valley,
A soil that sprouts nothing
For any of us.

Wind

A dry wind over the valley
Peeled mountains, grain by grain,
To small slopes, loose dirt
Where red ants tunnel.

The wind strokes
The skulls and spines of cattle
To white dust, to nothing,

Covers the spiked tracks of beetles,
Of tumbleweed, of sparrows
That pecked the ground for insects.

Evenings, when I am in the yard weeding,
The wind picks up the breath of my armpits
Like dust, swirls it
Miles away

And drops it
On the ear of a rabid dog,
And I take on another life.

Wind

When you got up this morning the sun
Blazed an hour in the sky,

A lizard hid
Under the curled leaves of manzanita
And winked its dark lids.

Later, the sky grayed,
And the cold wind you breathed
Was moving under your skin and already far
From the small hives of your lungs.

Stars

At dusk the first stars appear.
Not one eager finger points toward them.
A little later the stars spread with the night
And an orange moon rises
To lead them, like a shepherd, toward dawn.

Sun

In June the sun is a bonnet of light
Coming up,
Little by little,
From behind a skyline of pine.

The pastures sway with fiddle-neck
Tassels of foxtail.

At Piedra
A couple fish on the river's edge,
Their shadows deep against the water.
Above, in the stubbled slopes,
Cows climb down
As the heat rises
In a mist of blond locusts,
Returning to the valley.

Rain

When autumn rains flatten sycamore leaves,
The tiny volcanos of dirt
Ants raised around their holes,
I should be out of work.

My silverware and stack of plates will go unused
Like the old, my two good slacks
Will smother under a growth of lint
And smell of the old dust
That rises
When the closet door opens or closes.

The skin of my belly will tighten like a belt
And there will be no reason for pockets.

Fog

If you go to your window
You will notice a fog drifting in.

The sun is no stronger than a flashlight.
Not all the sweaters
Hung in closets all summer

Could soak up this mist. The fog:
A mouth nibbling everything to its origin,
Pomegranate trees, stolen bicycles,

The string of lights at a used-car lot,
A Pontiac with scorched valves.

In Fresno the fog is passing
The young thief prying a window screen,
Graying my hair that falls
And goes unfound, my fingerprints
Slowly growing a fur of dust—

One hundred years from now
There should be no reason to believe
I lived.

Daybreak

In this moment when the light starts up
In the east and rubs
The horizon until it catches fire,

We enter the fields to hoe,
Row after row, among the small flags of onion,
Waving off the dragonflies
That ladder the air.

And tears the onions raise
Do not begin in your eyes but in ours,
In the salt blown
From one blister into another;

They begin in knowing
You will never waken to bear
The hour timed to a heart beat,
The wind pressing us closer to the ground.

When the season ends,
And the onions are unplugged from their sleep,
We won't forget what you failed to see,
And nothing will heal
Under the rain's broken fingers.

Field Poem

When the foreman whistled
My brother and I
Shouldered our hoes,
Leaving the field.
We returned to the bus
Speaking
In broken English, in broken Spanish
The restaurant food,
The tickets to a dance
We wouldn't buy with our pay.

From the smashed bus window,
I saw the leaves of cotton plants
Like small hands
Waving good-bye.

Hoeing

During March while hoeing long rows
Of cotton
Dirt lifted in the air
Entering my nostrils
And eyes
The yellow under my fingernails

The hoe swung
Across my shadow   chopping weeds
And thick caterpillars
That shriveled
Into rings
And went where the wind went

When the sun was on the left
And against my face
Sweat   the sea
That is still within me
Rose and fell from my chin
Touching land
For the first time

Harvest

East of the sun's slant, in the vineyard that never failed,
A wind crossed my face, moving the dust
And a portion of my voice a step closer to a new year.

The sky went black in the 9th hour of rolling trays,
And in the distance ropes of rain dropped to pull me
From the thick harvest that was not mine.

Summer

Once again, tell me, what was it like?
There was a windowsill of flies.
It meant the moon pulled its own weight
And the black sky cleared itself
Like a sneeze.

What about the farm worker?
He had no bedroom. He had a warehouse
Of heat, a swamp cooler
That turned no faster than a raffle cage.

And the farms?
There were groves
Of fig trees that went unpicked.
The fruit wrinkled and flattened
Like the elbows
Of an old woman.

What about the Projects in the Eastside?
I can't really say. Maybe a child
Burned his first book of matches.
Maybe the burn is disappearing
Under the first layer
Of skin

And next summer?
It will be the same. Boredom,
In early June, will settle
On the eyelash shading your pupil from dust,
On the shoulder you look over
To find the sun rising
From the Sierras.

Sadako

The day the sparrows move south
The wind east

We will not see each other
Field workers gather like a bush
Of fog in the Westside
And those sleeping in the Mission unfold like chairs

Daybreak
The cloth awnings spread from storefronts
Chickens gutted and noosed on poles
In the unlit butcher shops

Where a door opens for business   the cold enters
With a little purse of dust
Where the cafe steams   a bus driver runs
A knife across his plate

Dusk   and what follows is this
The streetlights wink on
The newspapers porched   and a woman stoops over
Her dress raising like an eyelid
To the night

The sparrows move south with their eyes closed
The wind east

We will not see each other

Piedra

When the day shut like a suitcase
And left for the horizon

When the fog squatted in the vineyard
Like a stray dog

We fished there   Later we
Looked for soapstone   but found

A piece of the night rising from within us
And spreading among the cottonwoods

The dark water wrinkling
Like the mouth of an old woman whispering *Lord*

I pointed out carlights fanning past the orchard
Where the road narrows

Toward the collapsed bridge   My woman
Showed me a card of bark

The smashed bottles flaking back to sand
And farther away   near the road

Someone walking toward us—
My hand closed in my pocket

October

A cold day, though only October,
And the grass has grayed
Like the frost that hardened it
This morning.

              And this morning
After the wind left
With its pile of clouds
The broken fence steamed, sunlight spread
Like seed from one field
To another, out of a bare sycamore
Sparrows lifted above the ridge.

In the ditch an owl shuffled into a nest
Of old leaves and cotton,
A black tassel of lizard flapping
From its beak. Mice
And ants gathered under the flat ground
And slipped downward like water,
A coyote squatted behind granite,
His ears tilting
Toward a rustle, eyes dark
With the winter to come.

Avocado Lake

A body moves under the dark lake—
The throat is a tube of water, the hands
Are those of a child reaching for his mother.
It may be hours before the body rises
To the surface.

It is even longer before the body is found.
To blow breath in him is useless—
The lungs need to be wrung like sponge.
The gray film peeled like tape from the eyes.
The curled finger rubbed and kissed.

And now, at daybreak, the willows
Once again hold the heat, and a young girl
On the shore where a friend has gone under,
Skims pebbles across the lake,
Over what remains of him—
His phlegm drifts beneath the surface,
As his life did.

Moving

The sun goes down—
Heat rises from the grasses
Into what should be a moonless sky.

This hour, once again, the dry river brims
With a night that needs no current
To move west to the sea.

Street

para Ernesto Trejo

What I want to remember is a street,
A wide street,

And that it is cold:
A small fire in the gutter, cats running
From under a truck, their tails up
Like antennas. A short woman
With a short cane, tapping
Her way
Past the tracks.
                    Farther away,
An abandoned hotel
Whose plumbing is the sound
Of ocean. In one room,
A jacket forever without a shadow
And cold as the darkness it lies in.

Above, an angle of birds
Going south. Above the birds,
Clouds with their palms open and moving
Toward the Sierras.

Dusk: the first headlights come on,
And a Filipino stands
Under a neon, turning a coin
In his pocket.

Town

When you looked back
The blind whose pupils were just visible
Under a whiteness, and yet
Fading like twin stars,
Opened their hands

And you turned away.
The town smelled of tripe
Pulled from an ox
And hanging—
Smoke, fruit wrinkling
Or bearded with gnats.
The streets shone with rain.

After the rain
You wore the heat like a shirt,
You drank until your mouth
Hung open and no longer
Bothered to shrug off
The flies.

Later you laid under a slow fan.
You got up
To watch from the window.
A dog snapped
The ankle of a woman
Carrying bricks. She kicked it
And went on.

            Again you turned away
Afraid to think that it was night
And with the poor
You would sleep with spiders,
Dust in your throat
And sliding down.

The Level at Which the Sky Begins

Hunched in the green weather of a pine
Above a theater of steaming roofs
And all there was to see

I saw the sun take
Its first step
Above the water tower at Sun-Maid Raisin
And things separate from the dark
And lean on their new shadows

Through the streets
Cars fleeced in a light frost
Smoke lifting above the houses

A boy porching
The newspapers that would unfold like a towel
Over coffee   over an egg
Going brown   over the radio saying
It's 6:05   this is the music of America

Where the young got up hungry
Roosters cleared
What was caught in their throats
All night

Where a door slammed
A cane refused
The weight of the hand that carved it

On the horizon
Parting this hour from another
The shelved clouds pulled a cargo of rain
East into the full light that would soon fall
To meet us wherever we turned

3

In December

The dogs, the spotted dogs,
Fenced and barking,
Remain with me—
And the old face
Of a midget carting groceries
And muttering a rosary.

From town I went south,
Beyond the new
Freeway, searching.
In one house on Sarah Street
A doll's head,
Her nose chipped,
Facing the bedroom—
A broom was in there
But the floor went unswept.
If there was wind
The puffs of black lint
Would have rolled
Like tumbleweed
Toward their own
Particular deaths.
In the kitchen a draft
Moved like a housewife,
Reaching into cupboards
To find nothing
But vinegar
And an unstrung necklace
Of dead flies.

So long ago
The yard was gardened—
Tomatoes hanging
Like small red globes
And carrots poking
Into the kennel of earth;
On the line clothes lifted
With a slight wind.
And a child, perhaps,
Shaded by a cottonwood
And nailing on nailed two-by-fours
Or burning a shoe box
He imagines a hotel
And a lobby of people
Wanting out.

When I started home
Darkness was gliding west—
In a thin sycamore
Whose branches pointed
To a few stars,
Nests showed against the sky
And I felt a deepening
Like the night
Not yet an hour old.

Emilio

By now he is on the porch, alone.
His neck and wrists noosed in dirt
From the garden. His boots,
Twin animals smelling of crushed chinaberries
And mud, stand under the chair.
This evening, like all summer evenings,
The one cat soon to die with a yawn,
Comes meowing. The kids
That never catch cold and grow
Into manhood with pompadours
And alphabets of scars, roll worn tires
Through their street. Emilio watches them
Until night sends them home,
Out of breath and laughing.

*

A finger of moon points across his bed
And onto the wall, seeking the oval
Wedding portrait of Emilio and Ursula—
Their cheeks penciled pink in '39.
June bugs at the window and a gnat
Spins through the room.
He does not turn to these sounds
Nor stir from the heat
Beginning to lift like fog. He lies
Thinking of Mexico—a woman sweeping,
Farmland that suddenly rises
Into small hills of grass—
While the moon starts down
In a darkness that will not repeat itself.

History

Grandma lit the stove.
Morning sunlight
Lengthened in spears
Across the linoleum floor.
Wrapped in a shawl,
Her eyes small
With sleep,
She sliced papas,
Pounded chiles
With a stone
Brought from Guadalajara.

                    After
Grandpa left for work,
She hosed down
The walk her sons paved
And in the shade
Of a chinaberry,
Unearthed her
Secret cigar box
Of bright coins
And bills, counted them
In English,
Then in Spanish,
And buried them elsewhere.
Later, back
From the market,
Where no one saw her,
She pulled out
Pepper and beet, spines
Of asparagus
From her blouse,
Tiny chocolates

From under a paisley bandana,
And smiled.

That was the '50s,
And Grandma in her '50s,
A face streaked
From cutting grapes
And boxing plums.
I remember her insides
Were washed of tapeworm,
Her arms swelled into knobs
Of small growths—
Her second son
Dropped from a ladder
And was dust.
And yet I do not know
The sorrows
That sent her praying
In the dark of a closet,
The tear that fell
At night
When she touched
Loose skin
Of belly and breasts.
I do not know why
Her face shines
Or what goes beyond this shine,
Only the stories
That pulled her
From Taxco to San Joaquin,
Delano to Westside,
The places
In which we all begin.

41

Remedies

For a cough
Inhale the ashes of a pig's snout

For color blindness
Wash your brow where a peacock has drunk

For a canker
Large or small   sip the yoke
Of a turkey egg a thimble at a time

For a sty
Wink for every crack stepped on

Let Grandma come in without knocking
Let her light the taper whose smoke
Is a braid of white grass
Let her hang
The Virgin of Guadalupe
Above your bed

The tea she has brought is to be drunk
With a thick pucker   her rosary
Placed at your hands   It won't
Be long before the pain
Napping in you
Yawns and blinks awake
And Grandma hums   prays   hums

Copper

Leonard's wallet yawned open
And toothless, and the morning
Coughed from an empty shelf.
We walked dirt alleys after mass,
Collecting copper.
In the gravel yard, near the tracks,
We yanked out wire from the dashboards
Of buckled trucks, coiled tubing
And the short-throated pipes
Furred in oil. After selling
On the Westside, we went home
And napped where there was shade.

Today we are bloated on beer,
Glowing before a snowy TV.
Outside, snow slants into the street.
We laugh at nights we slept
Cold, in coats,
And I hugged a cat
That smelled like a broom—
Slugs laced the floor with silver.
If it were warm outside or we drunker
And swearing in the name of Christ
Or the Connie tattooed on Leonard's arm,
We would pick through an alley
Until we spotted the soft glow
Of copper, the only light needed
To show the way back.

Photo, 1957

In the one torn
Where your waist begins
You hold Debra
And look up,
Smiling to a cloud perhaps
Or a silver blimp
Pushing slowly against
The March wind.
You are 22,
My age now,
Your hair curled upward
Into a hive your
Man enters, your eyes
Twin pinpoints of light.
You do not know
In a few months
You will waken alone
And where
The rooms go unlighted,
It will be cold.
At dusk
The shadows of brooms
And backless chairs
Will pull southward,
Pointing the way
The dead vanish.

Then the house
Will tick like fire,
The cat circle
A table and refuse to lie
Flat, and in the yard
I will salt the slugs
Trailing the rain.

The Firstborn

All day the Nina sewed in this room
The curtain pulled down
But where it was torn
The sun flared
On the wall
And on the wall
The fingerprints
Of the firstborn
Who drowned face-up
In the basin

That was weeks ago   but still
She was frightened
When she washed
Or drank there
She thought of the baby
Coming up heavy
From the soapy water
His mouth open
On the cry
That did not reach
Humming   she
Toweled and hugged
Her little one
Before laying him
On the kitchen table
Back in the room
She stood looking
At the basin
And did not understand

What she was looking at
Or why   but then
Closing her eyes
Dipped her fists
In the water
And thought
Of her old town—
A rooster   the winter wind sliced
Through a reed fence

The Evening of Ants

I climbed into the chinaberry
With a play telephone
Rang for a taxi
To drive me away
And for a man to tighten
The leaky pipes
That shivered like our dogs
I rang mama
And hung up on her
Giggled   called again
To tell her I was hungry

Across a dirt yard
Chickens pecked at the broken glass
Winking with sunlight
And the Italian
Who would roll his Packard
A month later
Was alone on his porch   talking
Hours passed   birds passed
And those orange cats
Who eventually dropped
Under car tires
Moved as their shade moved

Evening neared
And the moment our father slipped
From a ladder   our mother
Reached the door
That opened into a white room

A white nurse   It was the moment
I came down from the tree
And into our house
Where a leash of ants
Swarmed for the rice   the cupboards   the stove
Carrying off what there was to carry
Between one root and the next

Spirit

When Grandma cried
Hugging the shirt
You stood in the room again
You saw her drop
To her knees
Kiss the rosary
And repeat prayers
Until a white paste
Gathered in the corners
Of her mouth
The next morning
Your cup and plate
Brimmed with cemetery grass
And the sofa
You gave Grandpa
Turned and faced south
We know you came back   father
And in the doorway
Leading to your bedroom
Wanted to fog
The family's photo
With the breath
You did not have
And years later
When your wife slept
With another
You waited
At their feet
Until they turned
From one another

Eyes closed
And sighing
Leaving them
A cupboard opened
The garage light
On and burning silent
As your jealousy
But was it you   father
Who sent me across
A dry orchard
Where I pointed
To a thin cloud
And thought
Beyond
That cloud
You lived in Limbo
God's Limbo
And were watching
And soon   for
The first time
You would come to me
Calling *son   son*

Moving Away

Remember that we are moving away   brother
From those years
In the same house with a white stepfather
What troubled him has been forgotten

But what troubled us has settled
Like dirt
In the nests of our knuckles
And cannot be washed away

All those times you woke shivering
In the night
From a coldness I
Could not understand
And cupped a crucifix beneath the covers

All those summers we hoed our yard
In the afternoon sun
The heat waving across our faces
And we waved back wasps
While the one we hated
Watched us from under a tree and said nothing

We will remember those moments   brother

And now that we are far
From one another
What I want to speak of
Is the quiet of a room just before daybreak
And you next to me   sleeping

Moving Away

Remember that you are moving away   sister
From what was a summer
Of hunger
And of thorns deep in your feet
Prayers that unraveled
Like mama's stockings
At the day's end
When she came back from candling eggs

Those small things you knew on the old street
Have vanished   a holly bush
And its bright jays
The rocks you scratched
From the yard
And were your dolls   blond dolls
Given heartbeats   names   legs
The sighs of those
About to cry
                Remember that you have left
Grandpa nodding like a tall weed
Over his patch of chilies and tomatoes
Left a jar of secrets
Buried in the vacant lot
On a hot day
And our family some distance
From your life
Remember

Braly Street

Every summer
The asphalt softens
Giving under the edge
Of boot heels and the trucks
That caught radiators
Of butterflies.
Bottle caps and glass
Of the '40s and '50s
Hold their breath
Under the black earth
Of asphalt and are silent
Like the dead whose mouths
Have eaten dirt and bermuda.
Every summer I come
To this street
Where I discovered ants bit,
Matches flare,
And pinto beans unraveled
Into plants; discovered
Aspirin will not cure a dog
Whose fur twiches.

It's 16 years
Since our house
Was bulldozed and my father
Stunned into a coma . . .
Where it was,
An oasis of chickweed
And foxtails.
Where the almond tree stood
There are wine bottles
Whose history

Is a liver. The long caravan
Of my uncle's footprints
Has been paved
With dirt. Where my father
Cemented a pond
There is a cavern of red ants
Living on the seeds
The wind brings
And cats that come here
To die among
The browning sage.

It's 16 years
Since bottle collectors
Shoveled around
The foundation
And the almond tree
Opened its last fruit
To the summer.
The houses are gone,
The Molinas, Morenos,
The Japanese families
Are gone, the Okies gone
Who moved out at night
Under a canopy of
Moving stars.

In '57 I sat
On the porch, salting
Slugs that came out
After the rain,
While inside my uncle
Weakened with cancer

And the blurred vision
Of his hands
Darkening to earth.
In '58 I knelt
Before my father
Whose spine was pulled loose.
Before his face still
Growing a chin of hair,
Before the procession
Of stitches behind
His neck, I knelt
And did not understand.

Braly Street is now
Tin ventilators
On the warehouses, turning
Our sweat
Towards the yellowing sky;
Acetylene welders
Beading manifolds,
Stinging the half-globes
Of retinas. When I come
To where our house was,
I come to weeds
And a sewer line tied off
Like an umbilical cord;
To the chinaberry
Not pulled down
And to its rings
My father and uncle
Would equal, if alive.

PITT POETRY SERIES
Ed Ochester, General Editor